GEMSTONE SECRETS A YOUNG WITCH'S GUIDE TO UNLOCKING THE POWER OF CRYSTALS

WILHELMINA WOODS

To all the young witches out there,
discovering the magic within themselves,
may this guide help you shine even brighter.
And to the crystals,
who have waited patiently for us to listen to their whispers
of wisdom
thank you for sharing your beauty and power with the
world.

Book Cover by Tukotuku Publishing

Illustrations by Tukotuku Publishing

First edition 2024

Print   978-1-991306-72-2

Ebook   978-1-991306-73-9

Contents

Unlocking the Magic of Crystals

Your Sparkling Adventure Begins!

H ey there, crystal-curious adventurers! Welcome to the mystical world of crystals, where beauty meets power, and nature's treasures unlock your inner magic! If you've ever been drawn to a sparkling gemstone or felt a curious tingle around a shimmering crystal, you're in good company. Crystals have been cherished for thousands of years for their healing properties, their ability to amplify energy, and the sheer wonder they bring into our lives. But they're so much more than just pretty rocks—they're powerful tools that can help you tap into your deepest desires, heal your heart, and connect with the magic of the universe. It's like having your own personal team of magical sidekicks!

In this guide, you're about to embark on an exciting journey filled with sparkle and wonder. Whether you're just starting your crystal collection or already have a few hidden gems stashed away, this book is designed to help you explore and unlock their full potential. Together, we'll dive into the magic of crystals and how you can use them in your everyday life to enhance your well-being, boost your confidence, and create your own unique spells. Along the way, we'll keep things fun, engaging, and, most importantly, totally relatable. You don't need to be an expert witch to work with crystals—just a bit of curiosity and a sense of adventure!

Why Crystals? Why Now?

You might be wondering: Why crystals? And more specifically, Why now? Well, crystals have always been here, patiently waiting for us to rediscover their magic. In today's fast-paced world, where life can sometimes feel like a whirlwind of school, friends, and social media, crystals offer a grounding force. They help us slow down, reconnect with ourselves, and tap into the energy of the Earth. It's like hitting the pause button on the chaos and finding a moment of peace and clarity.

Each crystal is like a little piece of magic from nature, vibrating with energy that can influence our emotions, thoughts, and even the atmosphere around us. They're like tiny powerhouses, each with its own unique personality and purpose. Crystals are unique because they come from the Earth's depths, formed over millions of years under intense heat and pressure. Each one holds its own vibration, and just like how every person has their own unique style, every crystal has a special energy signature. Some crystals are calming and help us find peace during stressful times, like a warm hug from a friend. Others give us the courage to chase our dreams and be bold, like a personal cheerleader in your pocket. The more you work with crystals, the more you'll discover how each one interacts with your own energy and how they can enhance your magical practice. It's like finding your perfect crystal squad!

How This Book Will Guide You: Your Crystal Roadmap

In the chapters ahead, we'll explore everything from the basics of choosing and caring for your crystals to creating crystal grids, performing rituals, and using crystals for healing, protection, and manifestation. But don't worry—we'll take it one step at a time. You won't need to memorize a ton of information or perform complicated rituals right away. This book is here to guide you at your own pace, giving you the confidence to trust your intuition as you work with these beautiful stones.

Each chapter is broken down into simple sections, packed with practical tips, real-life examples, and fun exercises you can try. We'll start by getting to know some of the most popular crystals—like Amethyst, Rose Quartz, and Clear Quartz—and dive into what makes them special. From there, you'll learn how to cleanse and charge your crystals (it's like giving them a spa day!), create powerful crystal grids, and even align your crystals with the moon phases and your zodiac sign. By the time you finish, you'll have built your very own crystal toolkit, ready to support your magical practice and personal growth. It's like having a toolbox full of magical solutions for whatever life throws your way!

A Personal Journey with Crystals: Your Unique Path

One of the best things about working with crystals is that it's a deeply personal journey. No two witches are exactly alike, and the way you connect with crystals will be unique to you. Some people feel an immediate connection when they hold a crystal, while others may take time to sense its energy. And that's okay! There's no "right" way to work with crystals—only the way that feels right to *you*. Throughout this guide, I'll encourage you to trust your intuition. After all, you're the expert on your own energy, and crystals are simply tools to help you enhance what's already inside you.

As we explore the world of crystals together, remember to have fun with it! Magic is meant to be joyful and empowering. Whether you're using crystals to calm your mind after a stressful day at school, attract positive energy into your life, or simply add a little sparkle to your room, they're here to support you on your path. The more you experiment and play with crystals, the more you'll discover how they can enhance not just your magical practice but your everyday life.

Setting Your Intentions: What's Your Crystal Wish?

Before we dive in, take a moment to think about what you hope to gain from working with crystals. Are you looking for more peace and balance in your life? Do you want to attract love, abundance, or confidence? Or maybe you're drawn to the idea of working with crystals to strengthen your intuition and enhance your witchcraft practice. Whatever your goals, setting an intention is a powerful way to begin your journey. Your intention will guide your crystal work and help you stay focused on what you want to manifest. It's like setting a destination on your magical GPS.

As you read through this guide, you might find certain crystals or practices calling out to you. Trust that instinct! Crystals are magical little beings, and they often find their way into our lives when we need them most. Whether you're new to the world of witchcraft or have been practicing for years, the power of crystals is a lifelong ally waiting to be unlocked.

So, are you ready to dive into the magic of crystals and discover the power they hold? Let's unlock their secrets and make some magic together!

The Magic of Crystals

Hey there, crystal curious! Whether you're already head over heels for their sparkle or just starting to wonder what the fuss is about, get ready for a journey into enchantment. Crystals aren't just pretty rocks—they're like tiny time capsules packed with ancient wisdom and energy, just waiting to help us unlock our inner magic and tap into the power of nature.

What's the Deal with Crystals?

So, let's break it down: what *are* crystals? In a nutshell, they're minerals that form deep within the Earth, growing in mesmerizing, repeating patterns. Think of them as Mother Nature's most intricate art projects, each one sculpted over millions of years. These unique structures aren't just for show—they give crystals the amazing ability to store and amplify energy, which is where their magical properties come into play.

Imagine this: from the moment they're born beneath the Earth's surface, crystals are soaking up all the vibes around them, like little sponges of energy. That's why they're so powerful—they've been holding onto this energy for centuries, patiently waiting for someone like you to discover their magic.

Crystals Through the Ages

Witches, healers, and wise ones throughout history have turned to crystals for their power and guidance. The ancient Egyptians adorned themselves with Lapis Lazuli for protection and wisdom, while the Greeks sported Amethyst to keep a clear head and avoid those nasty hangovers (smart move!).Crystal healing has been a cornerstone of Ayurvedic medicine in India for thousands of years. And across countless cultures, people believed that crystals could heal the sick, ward off evil spirits, and attract good fortune.

Crystals have never been just shiny trinkets. They've always been tools of magic and transformation, woven into the very fabric of myths and rituals across time. Even today, many witches consider crystals an essential part of their practice, using them for meditation, healing, and spellwork. They're like little power-ups from the Earth, ready to enhance our connection to the natural world.

Crystals & Modern Witchcraft

In today's witchcraft, crystals are like our magical sidekicks, each one with its own unique personality and purpose. Witches use them for all sorts of things: manifesting dreams into reality, creating a protective shield around themselves, finding emotional balance, and even sharpening their intuition. You can carry them in your pocket as a comforting talisman, wear them as jewelry to radiate their energy, or place them on your altar to supercharge your spells and rituals.

The beauty of crystals lies in their versatility. Whether you're setting an intention for the day, performing a sacred ritual, or simply seeking solace in meditation, crystals can amplify your energy and help you stay focused and grounded. Think of them as your personal cheer squad, always there to lend a helping hand when you need it most.

Crystal Energy 101

So, how do crystals *actually* work their magic? It all boils down to energy. Crystals vibrate at specific frequencies, and these vibrations can interact with our own energy fields. Remember that feeling of calm you get when you hold a smooth, cool stone? Your aura is intertwining with the crystal's vibrational field.

We are all stardust, woven from the cosmic tapestry of energy. Crystals, with their perfectly ordered atoms, vibrate at a steady, harmonious rate. When we come into contact with them, their vibrations mingle with our own, helping to bring us back into balance and alignment. That's why you might feel a sense of peace when holding Rose Quartz or a surge of energy with Carnelian nearby.

And here's the cool part: there's even a bit of science behind the magic! Crystals are used in everyday technology, like the quartz in your watch, because of their ability to maintain precise frequencies. In witchcraft, we tap into this same principle, harnessing a crystal's energy to influence our own vibrations and manifest our deepest desires.

Your Personal Crystal Connection

Now, here's where it gets really exciting: your connection to crystals is entirely your own. Some witches feel an instant spark with certain crystals, while others take a little more time to tune into their subtle energies. But the more you work with a crystal, the stronger your bond will become. It's like getting to know a new friend—the more you hang out, the deeper your understanding grows.

Let the crystal's vibrational essence wash over you. Close your eyes, take a few deep breaths, and simply be present with it. What sensations do you notice? Does it resonate with your soul? Each crystal will speak to you in its own unique way, and as you continue your journey, you'll learn to listen to these whispers of wisdom.

Choosing Your First Crystal

Ready to embark on your crystal adventure? There are so many beginner-friendly options to choose from! Amethyst, with its calming properties and ability to enhance intuition, is a great place to start. It's perfect for meditation and clearing your mind of any mental clutter. Rose Quartz, the stone of universal love, is another wonderful choice, especially for cultivating self-love and healing emotional wounds. And of course, Clear Quartz, the master healer, is a versatile crystal that amplifies energy and can be programmed for any intention you desire.

When it comes to choosing your first crystal, trust your intuition. It might sound a bit woo-woo, but sometimes, the crystal chooses *you*. If a particular stone catches your eye or feels good in your hand, that's a sign! Crystals have a way of finding their way to the witches who need them most.

Crystal Care 101

Once you've welcomed a crystal into your life, it's important to cleanse and charge it regularly. Crystals can absorb energy from their surroundings, so it's essential to clear away any lingering vibes that might not be serving you. You can cleanse your crystals by placing them in sunlight or moonlight, smudging them with sage smoke, or even burying them in the earth for a few hours to reconnect with their roots.

Charging your crystal is all about infusing it with your intentions. Hold your crystal in your hands, close your eyes, and visualize what you want it to help you with—whether it's protection, healing, or manifesting a specific goal. By setting a clear intention, you're programming your crystal to work in harmony with your unique energy.

You're Ready to Rock!

Now that you've got your first crystal and a basic understanding of their magic, you're ready to embark on a journey of self-discovery and empowerment. As you continue to explore the world of witchcraft, your crystals will become your trusted companions, always there to offer guidance and support. Whether you're seeking balance, protection, or a little extra sparkle in your life, crystals are a powerful tool in your magical toolbox. So go forth, embrace their magic, and let your intuition be your guide!

THE POWER OF EACH CRYSTAL

C rystals are more than just eye candy—they're like your magical sidekicks, each one brimming with unique energy and abilities. By working with different crystals, you tap into their special vibes to guide your intuition, heal your heart, and level up your spiritual journey. In this chapter, we're going to get up close and personal with three awesome crystals: Amethyst, Rose Quartz, and Clear Quartz. These gems aren't just pretty to look at—they're powerful tools every witch should have in their arsenal. Whether you're looking to dive deeper into meditation, attract more love into your life, or just boost your overall energy, these crystals have got your back!

Amethyst: Your Intuitive Guide

Let's kick things off with Amethyst, that gorgeous purple stone that's basically the "Intuitive Guide" of the crystal world. Amethyst is famous for helping you grow spiritually, sharpen your intuition, and bring a sense of calm to your life. It's like having your own personal spiritual mentor in a tiny, sparkling package. If you're the kind of person who wants to develop those psychic abilities or connect more deeply with your inner wisdom, Amethyst is *the* crystal for you.

One of the best ways to tap into Amethyst's power is through meditation. When you hold Amethyst during meditation, it's like clearing the cobwebs from your mind and opening up your spiritual awareness. Imagine this: you're sitting in a quiet space, holding your Amethyst in your hand, breathing deeply as its gentle vibrations help you focus and tune into your inner self. With Amethyst by your side, your mind feels clearer, your thoughts slow down, and you're able to connect more deeply with your intuition. For an extra boost to your psychic abilities, try placing it on your third eye (the center of your forehead) during meditation. This crystal is the perfect companion when you need guidance or clarity on a situation—whether it's figuring out the next step in your life or understanding the subtle energies around you.

But Amethyst isn't just for meditation—you can use it in your everyday life too. Keep a small piece by your bed to help you sleep soundly and remember your dreams. Lots of witches swear by Amethyst's calming energy for dealing with anxiety and stress. It's a great crystal to carry in your pocket or wear as a necklace, especially on days when you feel a little overwhelmed. You can even place Amethyst around your home or workspace to create a chill, balanced environment where intuition flows freely and peacefully.

Rose Quartz: The Heart Healer

Now, let's talk about the ultimate crystal for love and compassion: Rose Quartz. With its gentle pink hue, Rose Quartz is often called the "Heart Healer." It's the go-to crystal for all things related to love, not just romantic love, but also self-love, friendship, and compassion for others. If you ever feel like your heart needs a little TLC or healing, Rose Quartz is your BFF.

The magic of Rose Quartz is in its ability to open up your heart chakra, letting love flow freely into and out of your life. If you're looking to attract more love into your relationships or heal from past heartbreak, this crystal is a must-have. One simple but powerful ritual you can do with Rose Quartz is a self-love ritual. Hold your Rose Quartz close to your heart, close your eyes, and picture yourself surrounded by a warm, pink light. As you breathe in, imagine that light filling your heart with unconditional love and compassion for yourself. As you breathe out, let go of any negative emotions or self-doubt. It's a beautiful, gentle way to remind yourself that you are worthy of love and kindness.

Rose Quartz can also add a touch of magic to your everyday life. Wear it as jewelry to keep its loving energy close to your heart throughout the day. Rose Quartz can enhance the harmony and tenderness of your relationships. And if you want to boost the love vibes in your home, try placing Rose Quartz near photos of loved ones or in spaces where you spend time with family and friends.

Clear Quartz: The Master Healer

Finally, we have Clear Quartz, often called the "Master Healer" of the crystal kingdom. If you could only have one crystal in your collection, Clear Quartz would be the one to choose. It's like a magical multi-tool, amplifying energy, clarity, and healing. Think of Clear Quartz as a magical magnifying glass—it boosts the energy of any other crystal it's paired with, making it a super versatile tool for any witch.

Clear Quartz is especially powerful in meditation. It helps clear your mind and focus your intentions, making it easier to visualize and manifest your dreams. Imagine holding a Clear Quartz in your hand during meditation. As you breathe deeply, you feel the crystal's energy sharpening your focus, helping you to visualize your goals with crystal-clear clarity. Whether you're manifesting success, love, or personal growth, Clear Quartz can help you get laser-focused on what you want and how to bring it into your life.

Clear Quartz can boost the power of other crystals. Because it amplifies energy, pairing it with other crystals—like Amethyst or Rose Quartz—can make their properties even stronger. For example, if you're working on emotional healing, place Clear Quartz next to your Rose Quartz to intensify the loving, compassionate energy. Or, if you're deepening your intuition with Amethyst, use Clear Quartz to boost those psychic vibes. The possibilities are endless!

Caring for your Clear Quartz is simple but important. Like other crystals, it needs regular cleansing and charging to keep its energy at its peak. You can cleanse it under running water, leave it in the moonlight to recharge, or even use sage smoke to purify it. Keep your Clear Quartz energized, and it will be a reliable, powerful ally in your magical practice.

Embrace the Magic

These three crystals—Amethyst, Rose Quartz, and Clear Quartz—are powerful allies on any witch's journey. Each one offers unique magic, whether you're seeking spiritual growth, love, or healing. As you work with these crystals, you'll discover how their energies can support and guide you through all aspects of your life. Trust in their power, let their magic lead you on your path, and most importantly, have fun exploring the enchanting world of crystals!

CRYSTAL GRIDS FOR BEGINNERS

POWER UP YOUR MAGIC!

Alright, crystal enthusiasts, get ready to take your crystal game to the next level! If you thought your crystals were awesome on their own, just wait until you see what happens when they team up in a crystal grid. Imagine this: a magical network where the combined energy of multiple stones creates something way more powerful than any single crystal could achieve alone. It's like having your very own crystal crew working together, amplifying your intentions and turning your magical dreams into reality!

What Are Crystal Grids, Anyway?

So, what's the deal with crystal grids? Basically, it's like arranging your crystals in a special pattern, like a magical blueprint, designed to focus and supercharge their energy. These patterns are created with a specific goal in mind, whether it's love, protection, abundance, or healing. By placing your crystals in a geometric design, you're building a powerful energy field that helps you manifest your intentions faster and with laser-sharp focus.

Think of it like this: you're creating a crystal formation, and as you place each stone, their individual energies connect to create a circuit of pure power. It's like they're holding hands, amplifying each other's energy and creating a flow that's way stronger than any one crystal alone. This combined force works together in perfect harmony to help you achieve your magical goals. Pretty awesome, right?

The layout of your grid is just as important as the crystals you choose. You can start with simple designs, like a circle or triangle, and as you get more comfortable with grids, you can experiment with more intricate patterns. A basic circle layout is perfect for beginners because it's easy to set up, and the energy flows in a balanced way, like a magical merry-go-round. But don't stress too much about getting it "perfect." Trust your gut! Magic isn't about following strict rules—it's about what feels right to *you*.

When it comes to choosing your crystals for the grid, this is where your intention takes center stage. Let's say you want to create a crystal grid for self-love. You might pick Rose Quartz as your main crystal because it's all about love and compassion. Then, you could add some Clear Quartz to amplify that loving energy and maybe even throw in some Amethyst for spiritual wisdom and a sense of calm. Each crystal has its own unique vibe, and combining them in a grid is like creating a magical harmony of energies.

Creating Your First Grid: Let's Get This Party Started!

Now that you know the basics, let's dive into creating your very first crystal grid. The first thing you'll need is a clear intention. What do you want to achieve with your grid? Maybe you're looking to boost your confidence, attract positive vibes, or bring more peace into your life. Once you've got your intention locked in, it's time to choose your crystal crew.

Let's say you're setting up a grid for a confidence boost. You might pick Carnelian as your main crystal for its empowering energy. Pair it with Citrine for some extra positivity and a bit of Clear Quartz to amplify those good vibes. Once you've assembled your crystal team, it's time to arrange them into a grid pattern.

Find a quiet space where you won't be interrupted. Lay out your crystals in your chosen pattern, starting with the central stone—this is the captain of your crystal crew and represents your main goal or intention. Place the other crystals around it, creating a flow of energy that supports your intention. If you're working with a circular pattern, imagine the supporting crystals as evenly spaced teammates surrounding your captain.

Once your crystals are in formation, it's time to program your grid. Programming is like giving your grid its mission—infusing it with your specific intention. Close your eyes, take a deep breath, and focus on your goal. As you do this, place your hands over the grid, feeling the energy of the crystals beneath your fingertips. Visualize your intention flowing from you into the stones, like a magical current electrifying the entire grid. This step is all about focusing your energy and getting crystal-clear on what you want the grid to accomplish.

Now, it's time to activate your grid! Activating a grid is like flipping the switch and turning on the magic. One easy way to do this is to use a crystal wand (or even your finger) to trace the lines of energy between the crystals. Starting from the outermost crystal, trace a line towards the center stone, imagining the energy flowing through each crystal as you go. Feel the grid buzzing with power as you connect the stones. And just like that, your grid is ready to work its magic!

Advanced Grid Techniques: Leveling Up Your Magic

As you become more comfortable with crystal grids, you can start exploring more complex patterns and techniques. For example, you might create a more intricate grid based on sacred geometry, like a flower of life pattern or a star shape. These advanced designs channel energy in different ways and can be especially useful for long-term goals or bigger manifestations.

You can also supercharge your grid by combining it with other magical rituals. For instance, if you're doing a full moon ritual, you could create a grid to harness the moon's energy. Or if you're working on a spell for abundance, you can add a crystal grid to amplify the spell's power. Rituals like lighting candles, burning herbs, or reciting affirmations can all be paired with your grid to take its magic to the next level.

Sometimes, you might feel like your grid isn't working as well as you'd hoped, or maybe you're not feeling the energy as strongly as you'd like. That's okay! If something feels off, you can try cleansing and recharging your crystals, adjusting the layout, or even revisiting your intention to make sure it's super clear and focused. Crystal grids are all about intuition, and with a little experimentation, you'll find what works best for you.

You're a Grid Master in the Making!

Congratulations! You've just taken your first step into the amazing world of crystal grids—a powerful tool for any teenage witch looking to level up their magical practice. Whether you're manifesting your dreams, healing your heart, or simply working to stay balanced, grids are a fun and creative way to focus and amplify your intentions. With practice, you'll be creating powerful, intricate grids in no time, and unlocking even more magic along the way! So go forth, experiment, and let your crystal crew help you shine!

CRYSTAL CLEANSING AND CHARGING

SPA DAY FOR YOUR MAGICAL BLING!

C rystals are like tiny batteries of magical energy, constantly soaking up and giving off vibes from the world around them. That's awesome, but it also means they can pick up some not-so-great energy along the way—whether it's from your environment, other people, or even from working too hard in your magical practice. That's why it's super important to cleanse and charge your crystals regularly. Think of it as giving them a refreshing spa day, recharging their batteries, and bringing them back to their full, sparkly potential. If you're ready to learn how to pamper your crystals like a pro, let's dive into the magic of crystal cleansing and charging!

Why Cleanse Your Crystals? It's Like a Digital Detox!

Crystals are natural energy sponges. Just like your phone or laptop can get sluggish when it's overloaded, your crystals can lose their mojo if they're bogged down by unwanted energy. After all, they're working hard for you—helping with spells, absorbing negativity, and amplifying your intentions. Over time, this can leave them feeling "heavy" or even blocked. Cleansing your crystals is like hitting the reset button, clearing away any leftover energy so they can shine bright and vibrate at their highest frequency.

Imagine you've been using a piece of Black Tourmaline for protection all week, and it's been your trusty shield against negative vibes at school or with those *pesky* siblings. But now, the crystal is holding onto all that negativity, like a backpack full of emotional baggage. If you don't cleanse it, it might not be as effective the next time you need it. By cleansing the crystal, you're giving it a chance to let go of what it's absorbed and return to its natural, happy state—ready to be your magical bestie again.

Crystal Cleansing: Time for a Spa Treatment!

There are tons of ways to cleanse your crystals, and each method is as unique as the crystals themselves. One of the most popular ways is using water—rinsing your crystals under running water, like a stream or even your bathroom faucet, can help wash away any unwanted energy. But hold up! Not all crystals love water. Some soft stones, like Selenite, can dissolve or get damaged, so always check if your crystal is water-friendly before giving it a bath.

Another great cleansing method is salt. You can either bury your crystals in a bowl of sea salt or create a saltwater bath for them. Just like with water, some crystals don't play well with salt, so do your research first! If you're looking for a gentler approach, you can use smoke from burning herbs like sage or palo santo. Simply pass your crystals through the smoke, letting it cleanse their energy like a magical smudge stick. You can also let your crystals soak up some natural vibes by placing them in sunlight, moonlight, or even burying them in the Earth for a little grounding session.

How often should you cleanse your crystals? It depends on how much you use them. If a crystal is part of your daily routine or has been dealing with some heavy energy, it's a good idea to cleanse it more often—maybe even once a week. For crystals that you use less frequently, a monthly cleanse is usually enough. Trust your intuition! If a crystal feels sluggish or doesn't seem to be working its usual magic, it's probably time for a spa day.

Charging Your Crystals: Power Up!

Once your crystals are squeaky clean, it's time for the next step: charging them up! Charging is like replenishing their energy and making sure they're in tune with your intentions. Think of it as giving your crystal a power boost, filling it with the energy it needs to work its magic for you.

There are a few ways to charge your crystals, and one of the most popular is using sunlight or moonlight. Sunlight is awesome for crystals that thrive on fiery, energizing vibes—like Citrine or Carnelian. But be careful with delicate stones, as sunlight can sometimes fade their color. Moonlight, especially during a full moon, is a gentler option that works for almost any crystal. Leave your crystals on a windowsill or outside overnight to soak up the moon's soothing light, and they'll be charged up and ready to go by morning.

Another way to charge your crystals is through the Earth. Burying your crystals in the soil for a day or two lets them reconnect with their natural energy source. It's like giving them a cozy nap where they can rest, recharge, and get grounded. If burying them isn't an option, placing them on the earth or even on a houseplant's soil can have a similar effect.

Setting intentions is a key part of charging your crystals. After they've been cleansed and charged with sunlight or moonlight, take a moment to hold your crystal and focus on what you want it to help you with. Close your eyes, take a few deep breaths, and imagine your intention flowing from your heart into the stone. This simple act programs the crystal with your specific goal, empowering it to work its magic for you.

Crystal Care Tips: Keep Those Gems Sparkling!

Now that you know how to cleanse and charge your crystals, let's talk about some general care tips. Proper storage is key to maintaining your crystal's energy. You don't want to toss them into a drawer where they might get jumbled up and pick up stray vibes. Instead, consider keeping them in a special box, bag, or display where they can be organized and protected. If you have crystals you use for specific purposes (like love, protection, or manifestation), you can even store them in groups based on their use. Velvet pouches, wooden boxes, or even small glass containers work great.

When you're traveling with your crystals, be mindful of how they're packed. Keep them in a soft pouch or wrap them in a cloth to protect them from bumps and scratches. Crystals love to be near you, but they also need to stay safe on the go!

Remember, maintaining the energy of your crystals is an ongoing process. Over time, you'll get to know the energy of each stone and sense when it needs a little extra TLC. Listen to your intuition and don't hesitate to give your crystals some extra love. Whether it's a quick cleanse after a stressful day or a full moon recharge once a month, these small acts of care will keep your crystals—and your magic—flowing smoothly.

You're a Crystal Care Pro!

By developing a solid routine of cleansing, charging, and caring for your crystals, you'll ensure they remain powerful allies in your witchcraft practice. A happy, well-cared-for crystal is a powerful tool, ready to help you manifest your dreams and protect your energy. So go forth, shower your crystals with love, and let their magic shine bright!

CRYSTALS FOR SELF-DISCOVERY

UNLOCKING YOUR INNER MAGIC

Self-discovery is one of the coolest parts of being a Young Witch. It's like embarking on an epic quest to figure out who you are, what makes your heart sing, and finding the courage to follow your own unique path. And guess what? Crystals can be your awesome sidekicks on this journey, acting as both guides and mirrors, helping you understand your energy and emotions on a deeper level. When you're in tune with yourself, magic flows more easily, like a river finding its way to the ocean. So, let's dive into how crystals can help you uncover who you truly are, grow into the best version of yourself, and navigate life's twists and turns with confidence!

Understanding Your Personal Energy: You're Like a Mood Ring, But Cooler!

We all have our own unique energy—it's like an invisible signature that's constantly changing based on our emotions, experiences, and the people we're around. Sometimes, our energy feels bright and buzzing, like we could conquer the world! Other times, it feels heavy or out of whack, like we're dragging around a backpack full of bricks. This is where crystals come in. They're like emotional tuning forks—they vibrate with specific energies and help us understand what's going on inside us.

For example, if you're feeling overwhelmed and anxious, holding a piece of calming Amethyst might help you realize that your mind is racing because you're juggling too many things at once (school, friends, that *annoying* sibling...). On the other hand, if you're feeling sluggish or unmotivated, a vibrant Carnelian can give you the kickstart you need to get back on track. Crystals amplify and balance our emotions, making it easier to tune into our own inner world, like turning up the volume on your feelings.

Finding Your Crystal Crew: It's Like a Magical Friendship Bracelet!

Finding your crystal match is a fun and personal journey. You might feel drawn to a particular crystal without even knowing why—and that's totally normal! Crystals often choose *us*, matching their energy to what we need, even if we don't realize it at the time. The next time you're in a crystal shop, pay attention to which stones catch your eye or feel good in your hand. Don't overthink it—just go with your gut. Often, the crystal that resonates with you the most is the one that's meant to be your guide in that moment.

Once you start working with crystals, journaling your experiences can be a game-changer. Keep a small notebook to jot down how you feel when using certain crystals, how they affect your mood, and any cool insights you gain. This practice not only helps you track your emotional and energetic shifts, but it also deepens your connection to your crystals. Over time, you'll start to see patterns and understand which crystals are your go-to allies for specific situations. It's like creating a personalized crystal guidebook, just for you!

Using Crystals for Personal Growth: Level Up Your Life!

Crystals aren't just for understanding where you are—they're also amazing tools for helping you get to where you want to be. Whether you're setting personal goals, manifesting your dreams, or overcoming obstacles, crystals can be your cheerleaders on your journey toward growth and self-discovery.

When setting personal goals, it's important to get clear on what you want. Crystals like Clear Quartz are awesome for amplifying your intentions. Hold your crystal in your hand and visualize your goal, feeling the excitement and joy as if it's already happened. The crystal will boost that energy, helping you stay focused and committed to achieving your dream. Whether it's acing that test, strengthening your friendships, or trying out a new sport, having a crystal to support your goals makes the journey smoother and way more magical.

Manifestation is another powerful tool for personal growth, and crystals can supercharge this practice by grounding your intentions and sending your desires out into the universe. Rose Quartz, for example, is perfect for manifesting love and compassion—whether that's self-love or deeper connections with others. Green Aventurine is known for attracting abundance and opportunities, making it ideal for career or financial goals. To manifest with crystals, hold your chosen stone, focus on your desire, and say your intention out loud. Keep the crystal with you as a reminder that your goals are already on their way to becoming reality!

Of course, growth doesn't happen without a few bumps in the road. Sometimes, life throws curveballs at us, and that's when crystals can be especially helpful. Smoky Quartz is great for grounding and protection, helping you navigate tough situations with a clear head. If you're dealing with self-doubt, Citrine's bright, positive energy can give you the confidence to push through. Keep these crystals close when facing challenges, and they'll help you stay strong and focused on your goals, like a trusty sidekick cheering you on.

Crystal Meditation for Self-Discovery: Chill Out & Tune In

One of the most transformative ways to work with crystals is through meditation. Meditation is like pressing the pause button on your busy mind, allowing you to connect with your inner self and gain insights into your path. Crystals can deepen your meditation practice by amplifying specific energies and guiding your focus. If you're new to meditation, don't worry—it's all about finding what works for *you*.

For a basic crystal meditation, start by finding a quiet space where you won't be disturbed. Choose a crystal that matches your current goal or emotional state—Amethyst for intuition, Rose Quartz for love, or Clear Quartz for clarity. Sit comfortably, close your eyes, and hold the crystal in your hand. Take a few deep breaths, focusing on the energy of the crystal. As you breathe in, imagine the crystal's energy flowing into you, filling you with peace and light. As you breathe out, let go of any tension or negativity, like releasing balloons into the sky.

If you want to take your meditation to the next level, you can use your crystal for visualizing your future. Hold the crystal and close your eyes. Picture yourself a year from now, living the life you dream of—whether that's being more confident, achieving a personal goal, or simply feeling happy and balanced. Let the crystal's energy guide your visualization, making it feel more real and vivid. The more clearly you can see your future, the more likely you are to make it happen!

Crystals can also help with healing past wounds. If you're holding onto pain from a past experience, try using a stone like Rhodonite or Black Obsidian, both known for their emotional healing properties. During your meditation, imagine the crystal gently drawing out any lingering hurt or negativity, leaving space for healing and peace. Over time, working with crystals in this way can help you let go of old patterns and move forward with a lighter heart.

Crystals: Your Partners in Growth

In the end, self-discovery is a lifelong journey, but with crystals by your side, you'll always have powerful allies to guide you. Whether you're exploring your emotions, setting new goals, or healing from the past, crystals will help you unlock your inner magic and grow into your true self. So, go forth and embrace the magic of crystals—they're waiting to help you shine!

CRYSTALS FOR EMOTIONAL HEALING

YOUR MAGICAL MOOD BOOSTERS!

E motions are a huge part of being human, but sometimes, they can feel like a rollercoaster ride you didn't sign up for. One minute you're on top of the world, and the next, you're spiraling into anxiety or self-doubt. It's totally normal, but wouldn't it be amazing to have a little extra support during those emotional ups and downs? That's where crystals come in! They're like your emotional sidekicks, always ready to help you navigate those feelings, calm your mind, and boost your self-esteem. In this chapter, we'll dive into how crystals can be your go-to tools for emotional healing, helping you feel more balanced and empowered, no matter what life throws your way.

Identifying Emotional Blocks: Unlocking the Hidden Treasure

The first step in emotional healing is figuring out where you might be blocked. Emotional blocks are like those sneaky, unresolved feelings that keep popping up and holding you back, like a persistent pop-up ad you can't seem to close. Maybe you've noticed patterns—like feeling anxious every time you have to give a presentation in class or struggling to let go of past hurts. These emotional blocks can create roadblocks to feeling your best, and that's where crystals can step in and clear the path.

To identify these blocks, start by paying close attention to your feelings. Are there recurring emotions that you just can't shake? Do you notice specific triggers, like feeling stressed every time you face a test or feeling down when you're scrolling through social media? Recognizing these patterns is the first step to healing them. Once you've identified the blocks, you can choose specific crystals to help you work through them, like assembling your own emotional support squad.

For example, if you're dealing with sadness or heartache, Rose Quartz is a powerful crystal for emotional support. Known as the "stone of love," Rose Quartz helps heal emotional wounds by promoting self-compassion and forgiveness. If fear or anxiety is weighing you down, try working with Lepidolite, which contains natural lithium and is known for its calming properties. Selenite is another great option, as it clears away negative energy and brings a sense of peace and clarity, like a mental reset button.

Once you've chosen your crystals, it's time to create your emotional healing plan. This can be as simple as carrying your crystal with you, meditating with it, or placing it on your heart or third eye while you reflect on your emotions. Set an intention for healing, something like, "I am ready to release this fear and welcome peace." Crystals work best when you're clear about what you need from them, so take some time to connect with their energy and let them support your emotional journey.

Crystals for Anxiety and Stress: Your Chill Pill

Let's face it—stress and anxiety are part of life, especially for teenagers. Whether it's school pressure, social drama, or just feeling overwhelmed, anxiety can sneak up on you and ruin your whole day. Luckily, there are crystals that are amazing at soothing anxiety and bringing a sense of calm when you need it most. They're like your personal chill pill, but way cooler.

Lepidolite is one of the top crystals for stress relief. Its soothing energy can help calm those anxious thoughts and bring your emotions back into balance. Keep a small piece in your pocket or hold it in your hand during stressful moments—its tranquil vibes will help take the edge off, like a warm hug from your favorite blanket. Blue Lace Agate is another wonderful crystal for calming the mind. Its gentle, cooling energy is perfect for those moments when your thoughts are racing a mile a minute, and you need to slow down and find your center.

To make crystals part of your daily routine for stress relief, try setting aside a few minutes each day to hold your calming crystals and breathe deeply. You could start your morning with a quick meditation holding Lepidolite or end your day by placing Blue Lace Agate on your forehead while you lie down and relax. These little moments of crystal-powered calm can make a big difference in managing daily stress, like hitting the pause button on a chaotic day.

Another great idea is to create a stress-relief kit. Choose a few calming crystals—like Lepidolite, Blue Lace Agate, and Amethyst—and keep them in a small pouch or box that you can easily carry with you. Whenever you feel overwhelmed, you'll have your crystal kit ready to provide comfort and calm, like a magical first-aid kit for your emotions. You can even add a small sprig of lavender or a calming essential oil to your kit for an extra dose of relaxation.

Crystals for Building Self-Esteem: Unleash Your Inner Rockstar!

One of the most important parts of emotional healing is building self-esteem. Confidence doesn't always come easily, and it's something that many of us need to work on. The good news is that crystals can help you tap into your inner strength and boost your sense of self-worth. If you're feeling insecure or lacking confidence, Citrine and Carnelian are two powerful crystals that can help you unleash your inner rockstar.

Citrine is known as the "stone of success" because it radiates positivity and confidence. It's like a little ray of sunshine that reminds you of your worth and encourages you to go after your dreams. Carry Citrine with you when you need a confidence boost—whether it's before a big test, an important conversation, or just a day when you're feeling a little down. Carnelian, on the other hand, is all about courage and motivation. Its bold, fiery energy can help you tap into your personal power and remind you that you're capable of achieving anything you set your mind to. It's like having your own personal hype squad, cheering you on every step of the way!

To supercharge your self-esteem, try creating an empowerment ritual using Citrine or Carnelian. Light a candle, hold your crystal, and say a positive affirmation like, "I am confident, strong, and worthy of success." Repeat this affirmation while focusing on the crystal's energy. Let the crystal amplify your intentions and fill you with the belief that you are unstoppable. You can even place the crystal on your solar plexus (the area just above your belly button) to enhance its empowering energy.

Affirmations and crystals are a match made in heaven when it comes to building self-esteem. Choose an affirmation that resonates with you and say it aloud while holding your crystal. For example, "I trust myself and my abilities" or "I deserve happiness and success." As you speak these words, the crystal will amplify their energy, reinforcing positive beliefs and helping you embody that confidence in your daily life.

Crystals: Your Emotional Support Squad

In conclusion, crystals are incredible tools for emotional healing. Whether you're dealing with anxiety, building self-esteem, or working through emotional blocks, crystals can offer support, comfort, and guidance on your journey. As you continue to work with these magical stones, remember that healing takes time, and it's okay to be patient with yourself. Let your crystals be your allies in creating a more balanced, confident, and empowered version of yourself. You've got this!

CRYSTALS FOR MANIFESTATION AND ABUNDANCE

MAKE YOUR DREAMS COME TRUE!

Manifesting your dreams and desires is like having your own personal genie, but way cooler! Whether you're looking to attract love, success, or even just some extra cash for that new game you've been eyeing, the art of manifestation taps into the Law of Attraction. It's all about aligning your thoughts, energy, and intentions with what you want to bring into your life. Crystals can be your secret weapon for manifestation because they act like little amplifiers, helping you focus your energy and stay on track with your goals. In this chapter, we'll explore how to use crystals to manifest abundance in all its forms—whether that's wealth, opportunities, or even personal growth. Get ready to unleash your inner manifesting superstar!

Understanding Manifestation: It's Like Magic, But Real!

At its core, manifestation is about turning your thoughts and desires into reality. The Law of Attraction teaches us that like attracts like—what you focus on expands. If you're constantly thinking about abundance, success, and all the good stuff, you're more likely to attract those things into your life. But here's the catch: focusing on fear, doubt, or lack can bring more of *that* into your life too. That's why it's so important to keep your thoughts and energy aligned with your intentions. This is where crystals come in, like your personal cheer squad, helping you stay positive and focused.

Crystals are awesome at helping you stay in the right mindset for manifesting. They hold a stable energy that resonates with specific vibrations, and when you pair the right crystal with your intentions, it's like sending a super-charged signal to the universe. For example, Pyrite, often called "Fool's Gold," is a powerful stone for attracting wealth and abundance. Its bold, fiery energy encourages confidence and action, helping you manifest financial success, like scoring that dream summer job or finally saving up enough for that new phone. Similarly, Green Aventurine is known as the "Stone of Opportunity," perfect for bringing in new chances, career growth, and even those lucky breaks we all love. It's like having a lucky charm in your pocket!

Setting Your Intentions: Get Crystal Clear!

But before you start manifesting like a pro, it's essential to get clear on what you *really* want. Setting clear intentions is like giving the universe a detailed map to follow. Vague goals can lead to vague results, so the more specific you are, the better. Instead of saying, "I want more money," try something like, "I want to manifest $500 for my trip to the beach this summer." or even better, would be to clearly see your end result. What is it that you want the money for? If it is for a trip to the beach then just see yourself enjoying the trip to the beach, feel the sand beneath your feet, hear the waves in the background, feel the cool gentle breeze on your face. Now choose it. Choose that end result. Fix it into your mind and then ask yourself "What is the next obvious Step that I need to take?" And then do that. The clearer your intention, the easier it is for the energy to align and make your dreams a reality.

Creating a Manifestation Ritual: Let's Make Some Magic!

Now that you've chosen your crystal and set a clear intention, it's time to perform a manifestation ritual. Rituals help you focus your energy and create a sacred space for your desires to take shape. It's like setting the stage for your dreams to come to life! Here's a simple step-by-step guide to a manifestation ritual using crystals:

CHOOSE YOUR CRYSTAL: START BY PICKING A CRYSTAL THAT VIBES WITH YOUR GOAL. IF YOU'RE MANIFESTING ABUNDANCE, PYRITE OR CITRINE ARE GREAT CHOICES. FOR LOVE, YOU MIGHT CHOOSE ROSE QUARTZ OR RHODONITE. LET YOUR INTUITION GUIDE YOU!

SET YOUR SPACE: FIND A QUIET SPOT WHERE YOU WON'T BE INTERRUPTED. YOU CAN CREATE A MAGICAL ATMOSPHERE BY LIGHTING CANDLES, BURNING INCENSE, OR PLAYING SOME CHILL MUSIC. MAKE IT YOUR OWN SPECIAL SPACE.

HOLD YOUR CRYSTAL: SIT COMFORTABLY, HOLDING YOUR CRYSTAL IN YOUR HAND. CLOSE YOUR EYES AND TAKE A FEW DEEP BREATHS TO CENTER YOURSELF. AS YOU BREATHE IN, IMAGINE YOUR BODY FILLING WITH LIGHT, AND AS YOU BREATHE OUT, LET GO OF ANY DOUBTS OR FEARS, LIKE RELEASING BALLOONS INTO THE SKY.

VISUALIZE YOUR GOAL: FOCUS ON YOUR INTENTION. PICTURE YOUR DESIRE AS IF IT HAS ALREADY HAPPENED. SEE YOURSELF HOLDING THAT EXTRA $500, OR FEEL THE EXCITEMENT OF LANDING THAT NEW OPPORTUNITY. THE KEY IS TO IMAGINE IT IN AS MUCH DETAIL AS POSSIBLE, ENGAGING ALL YOUR SENSES. MAKE IT FEEL REAL!

SPEAK YOUR INTENTION: SAY YOUR INTENTION OUT LOUD, CLEARLY AND CONFIDENTLY. FOR EXAMPLE, "I AM ATTRACTING OPPORTUNITIES THAT WILL BRING ABUNDANCE INTO MY LIFE." SPEAKING YOUR INTENTION SOLIDIFIES YOUR DESIRE AND SENDS IT OUT INTO THE UNIVERSE, LIKE SENDING A MESSAGE TO THE COSMOS.

PLACE YOUR CRYSTAL: WHEN YOU'RE DONE, PLACE THE CRYSTAL ON YOUR ALTAR OR A SPECIAL SPOT WHERE IT CAN CONTINUE TO WORK ITS MAGIC FOR YOU. YOU CAN REVISIT YOUR CRYSTAL DURING MEDITATION OR WHENEVER YOU NEED A REMINDER OF YOUR INTENTION.

Supercharge Your Manifestation!

Crystals also work beautifully alongside other manifestation tools like vision boards, affirmations, or even journaling. If you have a vision board, try placing your crystal on it or near it to enhance the energy flow. When you say affirmations, hold your crystal to amplify the intention behind your words. These little actions can supercharge your manifesting process and make your dreams even more powerful!

Tracking Your Progress: Celebrate the Wins!

Manifestation doesn't happen overnight, so it's important to track your progress. One way to do this is by keeping a manifestation journal. Write down your intentions, the steps you've taken, and any signs or synchronicities that come your way. For example, if you're manifesting a new bike and suddenly start seeing bikes everywhere, that's a sign that your energy is aligning with your goal!

Revisiting your progress also allows you to make any adjustments to your ritual or approach. If a month has gone by and you're not seeing any movement, it might be time to re-examine your intention or try a different crystal. Sometimes, tweaking your mindset or breaking down your goal into smaller, more manageable steps can make all the difference.

Overcoming Manifestation Challenges: Don't Give Up!

Even with the best intentions, it's easy to hit roadblocks during the manifestation process. One common obstacle is doubt. Doubt weakens your energy and tells the universe that you're not fully committed to your goal. That's why it's crucial to stay positive and trust that what you're asking for is on its way.

If you find yourself struggling with doubt or fear, try working with crystals like Black Tourmaline or Smoky Quartz to clear away negative energy. These grounding stones can help you stay focused and keep your energy protected from self-sabotaging thoughts. It's like having a bodyguard for your dreams.

Sometimes, you might realize that your original goal needs a little adjustment. Maybe what you were asking for doesn't align with your highest good, or perhaps the timing wasn't right. That's okay! Manifestation is a process of trial and error. If you're not seeing the results you want, don't be afraid to adjust your approach or refine your goal. The universe is always listening, and sometimes a slight tweak is all you need to get things moving again.

Manifest Your Magic!

Crystals are powerful allies on the journey of manifestation, helping you align with your desires, stay focused, and overcome obstacles. By incorporating them into your manifestation practice, you'll find yourself better equipped to bring your dreams into reality. Trust the process, trust yourself, and watch the magic unfold! (And remember to always take guided action!)

CRYSTALS FOR SPIRITUAL GROWTH

LEVEL UP YOUR SOUL

One of the coolest things about being a witch is tapping into the deep well of spiritual growth. It's about understanding yourself on a soul level, connecting with the universe, and learning to trust that quiet inner voice—your intuition—that guides you through life. Crystals are like your magical mentors on this journey, offering support as you explore your spiritual path. They help you tune into your intuition, chat with higher realms, and access your inner wisdom—all while adding a little sparkle to your practice.

Enhancing Your Intuition: Trust Your Gut (and Your Crystals!)

Intuition is like your own personal GPS, guiding you through life's twists and turns. It's that gut feeling you get when something feels right (or wrong) without needing a ton of evidence. Developing your intuition is like learning a new language at first, but with practice, it becomes second nature. Crystals are your secret weapon for strengthening intuition because they vibrate at frequencies that align with spiritual insight and inner knowing. They're like little antennas, helping you pick up those subtle signals from the universe.

Lapis Lazuli, often called the "Stone of Truth," is a powerful crystal for enhancing intuition. It's connected to the third eye chakra, which is the energy center responsible for insight and psychic abilities. When you hold Lapis Lazuli during meditation or place it on your forehead, it's like opening a window to your intuition, making it easier to tap into those gut feelings. You might find that your dreams become more vivid, or you start noticing those little signs and synchronicities that guide you toward your goals.

Another awesome crystal for intuitive development is Labradorite, which is known for its mystical flashes of color. Labradorite is like the ultimate crystal for awakening your psychic gifts and protecting your energy as you explore the unknown. If you're ever working on a tarot reading, a pendulum, or any other form of divination, Labradorite can help sharpen your insights and protect you from any outside influences. It's like having a magical shield and a magnifying glass for your intuition, all in one!

To develop your intuition, start with simple practices using your crystals. For example, close your eyes, hold Lapis Lazuli or Labradorite, and ask yourself a question you've been pondering. Trust the first feeling or image that pops into your mind, even if it seems random or silly.

It might feel subtle at first, but with practice, you'll start to trust that quiet inner voice more and more. Crystals help amplify those subtle messages, making them easier to hear and understand.

Meditative journeys are another fun way to enhance your intuition. Try using crystals like Amethyst or Lapis Lazuli during guided meditations. Imagine traveling through a mystical landscape, meeting spirit guides, or receiving messages from your higher self. These meditative journeys, with the help of your crystals, can offer profound insights into your spiritual growth and path. It's like embarking on a magical adventure within yourself!

Connecting with Higher Realms: Chatting with the Cosmos

As witches, we're always reaching beyond the physical world to connect with the spiritual realms, whether that's through meditation, rituals, or just those quiet moments of reflection when we feel most connected to something bigger than ourselves. Certain crystals, like Selenite and Clear Quartz, act as bridges between our everyday reality and the higher spiritual realms. They help you raise your vibration, allowing you to connect with spirit guides, angels, or even the divine. It's like having a direct line to the cosmos!

Selenite, known for its ethereal glow, is one of the best crystals for spiritual communication. Its high vibration makes it perfect for clearing energy and opening up channels of communication with the higher realms. When you meditate with Selenite, place it near your crown chakra (the top of your head), and imagine it creating a column of light that connects you to the spiritual realm. You may start to receive messages in the form of thoughts, feelings, or symbols. Don't worry if it feels subtle at first—spiritual communication often starts as a whisper before it becomes a clear conversation.

Clear Quartz, the "Master Healer," is another crystal that can help with spiritual communication. It amplifies any energy or intention, making it ideal for channeling messages during meditation. You can hold Clear Quartz while asking for guidance from your spirit guides or while setting intentions to connect with higher beings. Its clarity reflects the clarity of the messages you'll receive.

Building a spiritual practice with crystals is all about consistency. You don't have to meditate for hours every day—even a few minutes in the morning or evening can make a huge difference. Start by choosing a crystal that resonates with you, like Selenite for communication or Clear Quartz for clarity. Sit in a quiet space, close your eyes, and breathe deeply while holding your crystal. Over time, you'll notice that your connection to the higher realms feels more natural, and your spiritual awareness deepens. It's like strengthening a muscle—the more you use it, the stronger it gets.

Crystals for Inner Wisdom: Unlock Your Inner Guru

Spiritual growth isn't just about reaching out to the universe—it's also about looking within. Crystals like Black Tourmaline and Amethyst are wonderful for helping you tap into your inner wisdom and uncover hidden truths about yourself. They act like a mirror, reflecting back the parts of yourself that need attention, healing, or celebration.

Black Tourmaline is an incredibly grounding stone, helping you stay connected to your inner self, even when the world around you feels chaotic. It's a great crystal to work with when you're seeking clarity on a personal issue or need help processing emotions. Hold Black Tourmaline in your hand and close your eyes. Ask yourself, "What do I need to know right now?" Let the energy of the crystal guide you toward your inner truth. Sometimes the answers are already within—you just need a little help accessing them.

Amethyst, with its soothing and spiritual energy, is another crystal for unlocking inner wisdom. It helps you see beyond surface-level emotions and thoughts, guiding you to the deeper layers of your soul's truth. If you ever feel confused or lost, meditating with Amethyst can bring clarity and peace. It's especially helpful during times of spiritual transition, when you're shedding old patterns and stepping into a new phase of growth.

Creating Your Spiritual Routine: Small Steps, Big Magic

Developing a spiritual routine with crystals doesn't have to be complicated. Start by choosing a crystal that resonates with your intention—whether that's Amethyst for clarity or Black Tourmaline for grounding. Incorporate it into your daily practice by meditating with it, carrying it in your pocket, or placing it on your altar. Over time, these small practices build up, helping you stay connected to your inner wisdom and continue growing on your spiritual path. It's like watering a plant—with consistent care, it will flourish and bloom.

Embrace Your Spiritual Journey

In the end, crystals are incredible tools for enhancing your intuition, connecting with higher realms, and accessing the wisdom that lies within you. Whether you're just starting your spiritual journey or deepening an existing practice, these magical stones will guide you toward a deeper understanding of yourself and the universe. Trust in the process, trust in your crystals, and most importantly, trust in yourself. Your spiritual journey is unique and beautiful—embrace it and let your inner light shine!

CRYSTALS FOR PHYSICAL HEALING

YOUR MAGICAL WELLNESS SQUAD!

When we think of healing, it's easy to focus on our emotions, energy, or even our spiritual growth. But let's not forget that crystals can also be your magical health allies, working wonders for your physical body! Whether it's helping you chill out, improving your sleep, or just promoting overall wellness, crystals are like your very own team of tiny healers. By harnessing their natural energy, you can create balance, enhance your well-being, and even use them alongside your regular health routine. Let's explore how crystals can support you in feeling your best, both inside and out.

Understanding Physical Healing: Good Vibes Only!

Crystals work on a vibrational level, affecting the subtle energy fields around and within your body. Each crystal vibrates at its own unique frequency, which can influence your body's energy systems, promoting healing and balance. Think of it like this: when your energy is flowing smoothly, like a clear river, your body has the power to heal and stay healthy. Crystals can help boost that natural process, especially when you're feeling drained, out of balance, or dealing with a physical issue. They're like little cheerleaders for your body's natural healing abilities.

For example, Hematite is a grounding crystal that's like a superhero for physical healing. Its energy is like a stabilizing anchor, helping to bring balance to your body and mind. Hematite is known to support blood circulation and detoxify the body, making it a great stone to carry with you if you're recovering from an illness or just need a boost of physical vitality. It's like having a mini-spa treatment in your pocket!

Another go-to crystal for physical health is Fluorite, a stunning stone that comes in a variety of colors, each with its own healing properties. Fluorite is often called the "health stone" because of its ability to cleanse and protect. It's especially helpful for boosting the immune system and clearing out toxins, like a magical shield and detoxifier all in one. If you're feeling run-down or fighting off a cold, Fluorite can help keep your body in balance and give you the energy you need to heal.

Crystals & Traditional Medicine: A Dynamic Duo

While crystals are amazing at supporting physical health, they're not a replacement for traditional medical care. Instead, think of them as working alongside treatments like medication, therapy, or rest to enhance your body's healing process. If you're dealing with a physical issue, you can place crystals near the affected area or keep them in your environment to support your recovery. For example, if you're experiencing headaches, try placing a piece of Amethyst on your forehead for its calming and healing properties. Just remember to always consult a healthcare professional when necessary—think of your crystals as the magical sidekicks to your regular health routine!

Crystals for Energy Balance: Chakra Power!

Our bodies are made up of energy, and that energy flows through us in patterns and centers, often called chakras. When your chakras are balanced and aligned, you feel vibrant, centered, and healthy. But when they're blocked or out of balance, it can feel like a traffic jam in your energy system, and you might experience physical discomfort, emotional distress, or low energy. Crystals can help keep your chakras in harmony by providing the right energy boost to each one.

Each chakra corresponds to a specific area of the body, and different crystals resonate with these energy centers. For example, Red Jasper is great for the root chakra (located at the base of your spine) and helps with grounding and physical strength. It's like having a solid foundation for your energy. Citrine, a bright and sunny stone, works wonders for your solar plexus chakra (just above your belly button), promoting confidence and personal power. It's like a little burst of sunshine for your soul! Meanwhile, Blue Lace Agate is a soothing stone for your throat chakra, helping with communication and self-expression. It's like having a clear channel for your thoughts and feelings.

To balance your chakras, try creating a healing routine that includes crystals. You can lie down and place crystals directly on each chakra, starting from the root and working your way up to the crown (at the top of your head). As you breathe deeply, imagine each crystal radiating energy, clearing away any blockages, and restoring balance. Even spending five or ten minutes with this practice can leave you feeling refreshed and centered, like you've just hit the reset button on your whole system.

Energy blockages can often show up as physical symptoms. Maybe you've noticed tension in your chest when you're feeling anxious, or a sore throat when you've been holding back something you wanted to say. These are signs that your energy isn't flowing as smoothly as it could be. Using crystals like Black Tourmaline or Clear Quartz can help break up those blockages and get your energy moving again, like clearing a path for a river to flow freely. By addressing these blockages early on, you can prevent them from turning into bigger problems down the road.

Crystals for Sleep and Relaxation: Sweet Dreams!

If you've ever tossed and turned all night, you know how important a good night's sleep is for your physical health. Lack of sleep can leave you feeling like a zombie, grumpy, and more likely to get sick. Luckily, there are several crystals that are perfect for promoting deep, restful sleep and relaxation. They're like a lullaby for your soul.

Howlite is one of the best crystals for sleep. Its calming energy helps quiet an overactive mind, making it easier to drift off to dreamland. If you often find yourself lying awake at night with thoughts racing through your head, placing Howlite under your pillow or beside your bed can help you relax and let go of the day's stress. It's like having a worry-eraser for your mind. Another excellent crystal for sleep is Amethyst, known for its soothing and peaceful vibes. Amethyst helps calm the mind, making it easier to fall asleep and even promoting more vivid and insightful dreams. It's like having a dreamcatcher for your subconscious!

To create a sleep ritual with crystals, start by placing your chosen stone (Howlite or Amethyst) under your pillow or on your nightstand. Take a few moments before bed to hold the crystal, close your eyes, and take a few deep breaths. Imagine the crystal's energy surrounding you like a soft, protective blanket, calming you as you prepare for sleep. You can also pair this with a relaxing affirmation, like "I am peaceful, and I release the worries of the day."

In addition to improving sleep, crystals can enhance your relaxation throughout the day. Try keeping a piece of Lepidolite or Selenite on your desk or in your living space to promote a sense of calm. When you're feeling stressed, hold the crystal in your hand, close your eyes, and take a few deep breaths. Let its soothing energy wash over you, helping you release tension and find a moment of peace in a busy day.

Crystals: Your Wellness BFFs

By incorporating crystals into your physical healing practices, you can create a more balanced and harmonious relationship with your body. Whether you're using them for energy balance, physical recovery, or relaxation, crystals are an amazing addition to your wellness toolkit.

They may not replace a doctor's visit, but they certainly add an extra layer of magic to your journey toward physical well-being! So, go forth and explore the healing power of crystals—your body will thank you!

CRYSTALS FOR RELATIONSHIPS AND LOVE

YOUR MAGICAL WINGMAN (OR WINGWOMAN!)

Love and relationships are a rollercoaster of emotions, and as a teenage witch, you might be wondering how crystals can help you navigate those highs and lows of romance, friendship, and connection. Whether you're crushing hard, trying to strengthen your bonds with your BFFs, or healing from a breakup, crystals are like your magical wingman (or wingwoman!), helping you create harmony, deepen your connections, and guide you through the emotional journey of love. Let's dive into how you can use crystals to add a little sparkle to your relationships and bring more love into your life.

Crystals for Attracting Love: Calling All Cupids!

If you're looking to invite love into your life, Rose Quartz is your go-to crystal. Known as the "stone of unconditional love," Rose Quartz is the ultimate crystal for attracting romance and opening your heart to new possibilities. It's like having a little love magnet in your pocket! Whether you're crushing on someone or simply want to radiate loving energy, Rose Quartz helps you feel more open, compassionate, and ready to receive love. Carry a piece of Rose Quartz in your pocket, or wear it as jewelry, especially when you're around your crush or going out on a date. It's like sending out a signal to the universe that you're ready for love!

Another powerful crystal for romance is Garnet. Garnet is all about passion, desire, and boldness—perfect for bringing some fire into your love life. If you're looking to deepen a romantic connection or spice things up, Garnet can give you the confidence and spark you need. You can place a small piece of Garnet under your pillow or near your bed to increase passion and attraction. It's like having a little love potion in crystal form! Just be careful not to overdo it—we don't want any accidental love triangles!

One of the most magical ways to use crystals for love is by creating a crystal grid. A love grid is designed to attract romantic energy and enhance your love prospects. It's like building a beacon of love that the universe can't ignore! To create one, gather a few love-related crystals—Rose Quartz, Garnet, and even Green Aventurine, which is known for bringing luck in love. Arrange them in a heart shape or a simple geometric pattern, with Rose Quartz at the center. As you set up the grid, focus on your intention, whether that's attracting new love, deepening a current relationship, or simply inviting more love into your life. Let the energy of the grid work its magic and open your heart to all the possibilities!

Strengthening Existing Relationships: Crystal Glue for Your Bonds

Crystals aren't just for attracting new love—they're also amazing for strengthening the relationships you already have. Whether it's with a romantic partner, a close friend, or even a family member, crystals can help bring harmony, balance, and understanding to any relationship. They're like the glue that keeps your bonds strong and healthy.

Amazonite is one of the best crystals for relationship harmony. Its calming energy helps soothe tensions and promotes open, honest communication. If you and your bestie have been butting heads or dealing with misunderstandings, Amazonite can help clear the air. Carry it with you during those tricky conversations or place it in the room where you spend time together to encourage peaceful vibes. Amazonite's soothing energy will help both of you feel more relaxed and willing to see things from each other's perspective. It's like having a mediator in crystal form!

Rhodonite is another great crystal for relationships, especially when it comes to strengthening those bonds. It's known as the "stone of compassion" and is excellent for fostering forgiveness, patience, and understanding in relationships. If you've been going through a rough patch with someone you care about, Rhodonite can help mend any emotional distance and remind both of you why your connection is worth fighting for. It's like a little hug for your heart.

To deepen your bond with someone, try creating a simple ritual using crystals. Sit down with your partner, friend, or family member and hold a piece of Amazonite or Rhodonite in your hands. Take turns speaking from the heart, sharing your thoughts, feelings, or what you appreciate about each other. The crystal's energy will help amplify the love and understanding between you, making it easier to resolve any tension and strengthen your bond. It's like a magical bonding experience!

Communication is key in any relationship, and crystals can help make those tough conversations a little smoother. Blue Lace Agate, known for its gentle energy, is the perfect crystal for enhancing communication. Whether you're having a serious talk or just want to improve everyday conversations with your friends or family, keeping Blue Lace Agate nearby can help you express yourself clearly and calmly. You can also wear it as a necklace or hold it during important discussions to encourage open dialogue and mutual understanding. It's like having a translator for your feelings!

Healing Relationship Issues: Mending Broken Hearts

Even the best relationships come with challenges, and sometimes, healing is needed. Whether you're working through a fight with your bestie, dealing with trust issues, or healing from a breakup, crystals can offer comfort and support during those tough times. They're like your emotional first-aid kit.

Chrysoprase is a wonderful crystal for forgiveness and emotional healing. Its gentle energy helps you release resentment and open your heart to forgiveness—whether you're forgiving yourself or someone else. If you've been holding onto hurt feelings or find it difficult to let go of past mistakes, meditate with Chrysoprase to help soothe your heart and promote healing. It's like a balm for your soul.

Another great crystal for emotional healing is Blue Calcite. This soft, nurturing stone is perfect for mending relationship wounds, especially when emotions are raw. If you're going through a breakup or trying to heal a broken heart, keep Blue Calcite close to help ease your emotional pain and bring comfort during tough times. It's like a warm hug from a trusted friend.

Sometimes, relationships can become toxic, and letting go is the best thing you can do for your well-being. If you're struggling to release a toxic relationship, Black Obsidian can help. Black Obsidian is known for its ability to cut through negative energy and provide protection. Hold a piece of Black Obsidian when you're feeling overwhelmed or stuck in a relationship that no longer serves you. Its powerful energy can help you find the strength to let go and move on, leaving behind what no longer supports your highest good. It's like a magical shield, protecting you from negativity and empowering you to move forward.

Crystals: Your Relationship BFFs

Crystals like Rose Quartz, Garnet, Amazonite, and Rhodonite offer not only love and harmony but also the tools to heal, strengthen, and grow your relationships.

Whether you're attracting new love, nurturing the relationships that matter most, or healing from emotional wounds, crystals provide gentle yet powerful support in all areas of love and connection. So, embrace the magic of crystals and let them guide you on your journey to deeper, more meaningful relationships. Remember, love is a beautiful adventure, and with crystals by your side, you'll always have a little extra magic to help you along the way!

CRYSTALS FOR PROTECTION

YOUR MAGICAL FORCE FIELD!

A s a teenage witch, protecting your energy is like having your own personal force field – it keeps you grounded, safe, and in tune with your goals. Whether it's shielding yourself from those pesky negative vibes (like when your sibling is being *extra* annoying), setting up boundaries at home or school, or keeping your energy protected while you're out and about, crystals can be your trusty sidekicks. They act like magical bodyguards, creating energetic barriers that deflect unwanted energy and keep you feeling secure. In this chapter, we'll dive into the different ways crystals offer protection, and how you can use them to shield yourself, your space, and your energy – wherever you go!

Understanding Crystal Protection: Your Energetic Armor

Crystals are like little energy transformers, interacting with the vibes around and within us. They can act like sponges, shields, or even mirrors depending on their unique properties. When it comes to protection, certain crystals vibrate at a frequency that's like a "do not enter" sign for negative energy. This is why witches have used protection crystals for centuries—to keep bad vibes at bay and stay grounded in their own power. The beauty of protection crystals is that they're always working in the background, quietly filtering out negativity and helping you maintain your emotional and spiritual balance. It's like having a 24/7 security system for your energy!

For example, Black Tourmaline is one of the most well-known protection stones. It's like the ultimate body-guard—powerful, reliable, and always ready to deflect negative energy. When you carry Black Tourmaline or place it around your space, it forms an energetic barrier that blocks unwanted energy from reaching you. Whether it's negative emotions from other people (drama alert!) or chaotic energy from stressful environments (hello, pop quiz!), Black Tourmaline has your back.

Smoky Quartz is another fantastic stone for protection, especially when you're feeling overwhelmed or anxious. Its grounding energy not only shields you from negative influences, but it also transforms those bad vibes into something more positive. It's perfect for when you're feel-ing stressed, providing a calming effect while keeping you protected. It's like a warm hug and a shield all rolled into one!

And if you're looking for something strong and fierce, Obsidian is your go-to crystal. This volcanic glass crystal is like a psychic shield, protecting you from energy vampires (you know, those people who always seem to drain your energy) and unwanted spiritual attacks. It's like having a magical force field around you.

To make your crystal's protective power even stronger, it's important to program it with your specific intention. Hold the crystal in your hand, close your eyes, and focus on the kind of protection you want. Visualize the crystal forming a glowing shield around you, deflecting any negative energy that comes your way. This act of programming is like giving your crystal a pep talk, reminding it of its important mission to protect you.

Protecting Your Space: Creating a Safe Haven

It's not just your personal energy that needs protection – your home, bedroom, or even your locker at school can benefit from the protective power of crystals. Setting up crystal boundaries in your space is like creating an energetic force field, one that keeps your environment clear and safe from unwanted energies. It's especially helpful if you live in a chaotic household, share a room with siblings, or simply want to create a sanctuary where you can recharge and be yourself.

A great way to start is by placing crystals like Black Tourmaline or Smoky Quartz at the entrances of your space, like by your door or windows. This creates a protective barrier that stops negative energy from entering, like a magical "keep out" sign. You can also keep a piece of Selenite in your room. Selenite is like a spiritual air freshener, constantly clearing and purifying the energy in the room. It also raises the vibration of your space, making it feel more peaceful and uplifting. It's like a spa day for your room!

If you want to take your protection game to the next level, consider creating a crystal protection grid. A grid is a pattern of crystals arranged with the specific intention of creating an energetic shield. For home protection, you can create a grid using Black Tourmaline, Obsidian, and Clear Quartz. Place a piece of Black Tourmaline in each corner of your room or home to create a shield around the space. You can add Clear Quartz to amplify the protective energy and Obsidian to provide that extra layer of strong, grounded protection. As you set up the grid, visualize the energy of the crystals connecting and forming a powerful barrier around your space. This grid will keep negative energy out and maintain a calm, protective atmosphere, like a cozy blanket of good vibes.

Protection on the Go: Your Portable Shield

Your personal energy is precious, and it's just as important to protect yourself when you're out and about. Whether you're traveling, going to school, or just running errands, carrying protective crystals with you can help you feel grounded and safe in any environment. It's like having a portable shield that you can take anywhere!

Traveling, in particular, can expose you to a lot of different energies—whether it's the stress of airports and train stations or the unfamiliar energy of new places. Carrying a travel-sized Black Tourmaline or Smoky Quartz in your pocket or bag can provide a sense of security and help shield you from energetic overwhelm. If you want something small and discreet, try wearing a crystal as jewelry. A necklace or bracelet made of protective stones like Obsidian or Hematite acts as a wearable shield, keeping your energy protected no matter where you go. It's like having a fashion statement and a magical bodyguard all in one.

Another fun way to carry your protection with you is by crafting your own crystal amulet or talisman. Choose a crystal that resonates with your intention—like Black Tourmaline for grounding or Labradorite for psychic protection—and wrap it in wire, thread, or fabric to create a personal charm. Wear it or carry it with you for an extra layer of magical protection wherever you go. It's like having a personalized lucky charm that also doubles as a powerful protector!

Daily Protection Rituals: Power Up Your Shield!

Incorporating protection rituals into your daily routine is a great way to make sure you're keeping your energy clear and protected. Every morning, before you head out, take a moment to hold your protective crystal and set your intention for the day. Imagine a bubble of protective light surrounding you, and visualize the crystal's energy strengthening that shield. Throughout the day, if you feel your energy being drained or notice negative vibes creeping in, take a deep breath, hold your crystal, and reconnect with its protective energy. This simple practice will help you stay grounded and shielded from unwanted energy, no matter what the day throws your way.

Crystals: Your Protection Squad

Crystals like Black Tourmaline, Smoky Quartz, and Obsidian are your ultimate allies when it comes to protection. Whether you're shielding your personal energy, protecting your space, or safeguarding yourself on the go, these powerful stones are always ready to help you feel secure, grounded, and safe. By integrating protective crystals into your daily life, you can create an energetic shield that keeps you balanced, focused, and free from negativity. So grab your favorite protection crystal, set your intentions, and let the magic of crystals keep you protected wherever you go!

CRYSTALS AND YOUR ZODIAC SIGN

IT'S WRITTEN IN THE STARS!

Ever wonder why certain crystals seem to whisper your name, while others just feel "meh"? Well, the answer might be hidden in the cosmos—literally! Your zodiac sign plays a big role in the energy you vibe with, and each sign has its own unique connection to certain crystals. Whether you're a fiery Aries, a grounded Taurus, or a dreamy Pisces, astrology can help you find the perfect crystals to boost your natural strengths and keep your energy in balance. In this chapter, we'll explore the magical link between your zodiac sign and crystals, and how you can use this cosmic connection to level up your witchcraft.

The Zodiac & Crystals: It's a Match Made in the Heavens

Just like the planets influence our moods, personalities, and life paths, they also have a say in the crystals we connect with. Crystals hold specific energies, and each zodiac sign is ruled by certain elements—Earth, Fire, Air, or Water—that determine which crystals will best vibe with your astrological energy. It's like finding your perfect match in the crystal world!

For example, Earth signs like Taurus and Capricorn tend to resonate with grounding crystals that promote stability, like a cozy blanket for their energy. On the other hand, Fire signs like Aries and Leo thrive with crystals that amplify their bold, dynamic energy, like a shot of espresso for their spirit. When you find crystals that match your zodiac energy, it's like unlocking a secret code to your magical potential. You'll feel more in tune with the crystal's power, and they'll help you unleash the strengths of your sign.

Elemental Magic: Find Your Crystal Tribe

To make things even more interesting, each element—Earth, Fire, Air, and Water—has its own set of crystals that boost the natural qualities of that element. Earth signs benefit from grounding stones like Hematite and Jasper, which help stabilize their practical energy. Fire signs vibe with Carnelian and Sunstone, which ignite their passion and creativity. Air signs connect with intellectual, light-as-air stones like Sodalite and Citrine, while Water signs feel at home with calming, emotional stones like Moonstone and Aquamarine. It's like finding your crystal tribe!

When choosing crystals based on your zodiac sign, remember to trust your instincts. Your astrological chart is a map of your personality, but you're the one who knows yourself best. If you're a Taurus who feels a strong pull toward the fiery energy of Carnelian, go for it! Your intuition is your most powerful guide, so listen to what your heart tells you.

Crystals for Fire Signs (Aries, Leo, Sagittarius): Ignite Your Inner Flame!

Fire signs are all about passion, excitement, and taking action. These are the zodiac's natural leaders, the ones who jump into challenges headfirst and thrive on the thrill of new experiences. If you're a Fire sign, crystals that match your fiery energy will help you tap into your inner confidence and drive. They're like a boost of rocket fuel for your spirit!

Carnelian is the go-to crystal for amplifying that fire energy. Known as the "stone of courage," Carnelian boosts confidence, creativity, and motivation. It's the perfect crystal for when you need to tackle a big project, like that science fair presentation or ace that audition, or take a bold step in your life, like asking your crush to the dance. For Leos, who are ruled by the sun, Sunstone is another must-have. It radiates positivity and helps you shine your light, making it ideal for boosting self-expression and leadership. It's like having your own personal spotlight!

But let's be real—being a Fire sign can sometimes mean burning a little *too* bright. When you're feeling overwhelmed or stressed, soothing crystals like Blue Lace Agate or Aquamarine can help balance your intense energy. Blue Lace Agate is perfect for calming those fiery emotions, helping you stay cool and collected even when things get heated. Aquamarine, with its calming water vibes, brings emotional balance and clarity, making it a great crystal to turn to when you need to chill out after a stressful day. It's like a refreshing dip in a cool pool on a hot summer day.

Fire signs can also create special rituals using crystals to amplify their natural strengths. A simple fire sign ritual could involve placing a piece of Carnelian or Sunstone under the sun for a few hours to charge it with solar energy. Then, during a moment of meditation or reflection, hold the crystal in your hand and visualize the warmth of the sun filling you with confidence, creativity, and power. This ritual can help you reconnect with your fiery energy whenever you need a boost.

Crystals for Earth Signs (Taurus, Virgo, Capricorn): Get Grounded & Grow!

Earth signs are the zodiac's stabilizers. You're practical, reliable, and deeply connected to the physical world. As an Earth sign, you tend to thrive when you feel grounded and secure, and crystals that resonate with the Earth element help you stay centered and productive. They're like a sturdy pair of boots, keeping you firmly planted on the ground.

Hematite is a grounding powerhouse for Earth signs. It helps you stay rooted, even during times of chaos, and it's perfect for when you need to feel more connected to the present moment. Whether you're a Capricorn focusing on long-term goals or a Virgo working through a detailed task, Hematite can help you stay focused and balanced. It's like having a personal anchor to keep you from drifting away.

Jasper, another great crystal for Earth signs, is known for its nurturing energy. It's especially helpful for Taurus, who thrives in stable, comfortable environments. Jasper's grounding properties make it a perfect crystal to keep with you when you're working on projects or need a little extra support in staying productive. It's like a warm hug from Mother Earth.

When it comes to boosting your Earth sign qualities, Pyrite is the crystal for success and abundance. Pyrite's golden shine is associated with prosperity, and its energy encourages focus, determination, and productivity. Whether you're manifesting financial success or working toward a personal goal, keeping a piece of Pyrite on your desk or in your workspace can help you stay motivated and attract the success you seek. It's like having a little cheerleader for your ambitions!

To enhance your connection with these crystals, Earth signs can incorporate them into a grounding ritual. For example, you might create a simple Earth altar by placing crystals like Hematite and Jasper alongside natural elements like soil, leaves, or flowers. Sit quietly in front of the altar, hold your crystals, and visualize roots growing from your feet into the Earth, grounding you in strength and stability. This ritual can help you feel more connected to your element and boost your productivity and sense of security. It's like recharging your batteries with the Earth's energy.

Embrace Your Cosmic Connection!

No matter your sign, working with crystals that resonate with your zodiac energy can help you unlock your full potential. Whether you're a passionate Fire sign, a grounded Earth sign, or somewhere in between, there's a crystal out there that will amplify your natural strengths and help you find balance. Embrace the magic of the stars, trust your intuition, and let crystals guide you on your journey!

CRYSTALS AND THE MOON

HARNESSING THE POWER OF LUNAR MAGIC!

T he moon has always been a source of wonder and magic, casting its spell on witches and dreamers for centuries. Its phases—new, waxing, full, and waning—each carry their own unique energy, guiding us through cycles of intention-setting, manifestation, reflection, and release. It's like the moon is whispering secrets to us, helping us tap into the natural rhythms of the universe.

But did you know that crystals are also deeply connected to the moon's energy? Just like the tides ebb and flow with the moon's pull, crystals are affected by its gravitational forces, and their energy waxes and wanes alongside the lunar phases. In this chapter, we'll explore the magical link between crystals and the moon, and how you can harness that lunar energy to charge your crystals, boost your rituals, and deepen your spiritual practice. It's like having the moon as your magical co-pilot!

Crystals & the Lunar Cycle: It's a Cosmic Dance

Crystals and the moon share a deep, natural connection. They're both born from the Earth's elements, and both carry energy that shifts and changes with the lunar cycle. Just like witches use the moon phases for different types of magic—setting intentions during the new moon or celebrating abundance during the full moon—crystals are even more powerful when they're synced with the moon's energy. It's like they're dancing to the same cosmic beat!

Each lunar phase has its own unique vibe that enhances the power of specific crystals. For example, the new moon, which symbolizes new beginnings and fresh starts, is a perfect time to work with Moonstone. Moonstone is known for its connection to the moon and its ability to heighten intuition, making it ideal for setting powerful intentions and manifesting your dreams as the moon begins to grow. It's like planting seeds of intention under the new moon's light.

During the full moon, the energy is at its peak, making it a time for celebration, gratitude, and letting go of what no longer serves you. Selenite, a high-vibration crystal that radiates pure energy, is often associated with the full moon. It's the perfect crystal to use when you want to cleanse your energy and release anything that's holding you back. Place a piece of Selenite near your bed or in your sacred space during the full moon to amplify your intentions and harness the moon's full power. It's like a cosmic reset button for your soul!

Incorporating crystals into your lunar magic can be as simple as adding them to your moon rituals. For example, if you're performing a new moon ritual, place a Moonstone in your circle to enhance your connection to your intentions. During the full moon, use Selenite to cleanse your energy and the space around you, ensuring that the energy you release is fully transformed. By aligning your crystal work with the lunar cycle, you're tapping into a powerful force that amplifies your magic and brings your intentions to life. It's like having the moon as your magical backup dancer!

Charging Crystals by the Moon: Moonlight Bath Time!

Charging crystals by the moon is one of the most powerful and magical ways to cleanse and recharge their energy. The moon's light acts like a reset button, washing away any stagnant energy your crystals may have absorbed and infusing them with fresh, lunar energy. While you can charge your crystals during any phase of the moon, the full moon is by far the best time for a deep cleanse and recharge. It's like giving your crystals a spa day under the moonlight!

To charge your crystals, simply place them outside under the moonlight or on a windowsill where the moon's rays can reach them. You can leave them out overnight, allowing the moon's energy to work its magic. Some witches like to add a little extra pizzazz to the ritual by creating a small crystal grid or placing their crystals on a piece of cloth or a plate with a specific intention written underneath. The key is to focus on what you want your crystals to absorb during this lunar charging session—whether it's clarity, healing, protection, or abundance. It's like sending your crystals on a moonlit mission!

A Full Moon Charging Ritual: Let's Glow!

Here's a step-by-step ritual for full moon charging that's easy and fun:

GATHER YOUR CRYSTALS AND BRING THEM TO A SPACE WHERE THEY'LL BE EXPOSED TO THE MOONLIGHT. YOUR BACKYARD, A BALCONY, OR EVEN A WINDOWSILL WILL WORK!

CLEANSE EACH CRYSTAL WITH SMOKE FROM BURNING SAGE OR INCENSE TO CLEAR AWAY ANY LINGERING ENERGY. IT'S LIKE GIVING THEM A QUICK PRE-SPA CLEANSE.

SET AN INTENTION FOR YOUR CRYSTALS. YOU CAN SAY SOMETHING LIKE, "I CHARGE THESE CRYSTALS WITH THE ENERGY OF THE FULL MOON TO BRING CLARITY AND STRENGTH INTO MY LIFE."

LAY YOUR CRYSTALS OUT IN A PATTERN THAT FEELS MEANINGFUL TO YOU. YOU CAN GET CREATIVE HERE!

LET THEM BATHE IN THE MOONLIGHT OVERNIGHT. IT'S LIKE A SLUMBER PARTY FOR YOUR CRYSTALS!

THE NEXT MORNING, COLLECT YOUR CRYSTALS AND THANK THE MOON FOR ITS ENERGY. GRATITUDE IS KEY!

Charging your crystals under the moon doesn't just refresh their energy—it also strengthens your connection to them. You'll find that the more you work with the lunar cycle, the more attuned you'll become to the rhythms of your crystals, your body, and the moon itself. It's like becoming part of a cosmic symphony!

Crystals for Lunar Energy: Channel the Moon's Magic

Crystals aren't just for charging under the moon—they also carry their own lunar energy, making them powerful tools for enhancing intuition, dreams, and emotional balance.

One of the best crystals for tapping into lunar energy is Labradorite. Known as the "stone of magic," Labradorite is deeply connected to the moon's mystical, intuitive side. Its iridescent flashes of color are like the moon's light shimmering through the night sky, and it's perfect for enhancing psychic abilities and encouraging vivid dreams. If you're working on dream recall or want to explore your subconscious, keep a piece of Labradorite under your pillow to open the gateway to your inner world. It's like having a dream portal in your bedroom!

Moonstone, as you might guess, is another must-have crystal for working with lunar energy. It's known for its ability to balance emotions and enhance intuition, making it ideal for times when the moon's energy feels overwhelming or intense. Moonstone works in harmony with the waxing and waning cycles of the moon, helping you ride the emotional waves with grace and ease. If you're feeling particularly emotional during a full moon, hold a piece of Moonstone and focus on its calming energy as you breathe deeply, allowing it to bring balance and peace. It's like having a moonlit meditation buddy!

You can also use crystals like Amethyst and Celestite to enhance your moon magic meditations. To connect with lunar energy, try a guided meditation where you hold a crystal in your hand, close your eyes, and imagine the moon's light shining down on you, filling your body with pure, white light. As you breathe in, imagine that light filling your heart and mind, bringing clarity and intuitive insight. As you exhale, let go of any tension or emotional heaviness, releasing it to the moon for transformation. It's like a cosmic cleanse for your soul.

Embrace the Lunar Magic!

By working with crystals and the moon, you're tuning into one of the most powerful forces in the universe. The moon's cycles guide us through periods of growth, reflection, and release, and crystals help amplify that energy, making your magical practice even more potent. Whether you're charging your crystals under the full moon or using them in your moon rituals, you'll find that the moon's energy enhances everything you do. Trust the power of the moon and your crystals, and watch your magic grow!

CREATING YOUR CRYSTAL TOOLKIT

BUILDING YOUR MAGICAL DREAM TEAM!

As a teenage witch, one of the most exciting parts of your journey is building your own magical toolkit. It's like assembling your very own superhero squad, but instead of capes and masks, you've got crystals! These powerful stones hold ancient wisdom and energies that can amplify your spells, enhance your rituals, and bring clarity to your everyday life. It's like having a team of tiny, sparkly allies, each with their own unique superpowers.

In this chapter, we'll walk through the basics of creating a crystal toolkit that's as unique and awesome as you are. From choosing essential crystals to incorporating them into your witchcraft, we've got you covered. Whether you're just starting out or looking to level up your practice, you'll discover how to curate a collection that's uniquely yours, filled with magical potential. So, let's get started!

Building a Basic Crystal Collection: The Must-Haves

When it comes to building your crystal toolkit, it's all about starting with the essentials. You don't need a gazillion crystals to begin with—in fact, a few versatile and powerful stones are enough to get you started. Think of them as the core members of your magical team, ready to tackle any challenge. Let's explore a few must-have crystals that every witch should have in their collection:

CLEAR QUARTZ: KNOWN AS THE "MASTER HEALER," CLEAR QUARTZ IS LIKE THE SWISS ARMY KNIFE OF CRYSTALS. IT CAN AMPLIFY THE ENERGY OF OTHER CRYSTALS, MAKING IT A STAPLE IN ANY COLLECTION. IT'S PERFECT FOR CLARITY, INTENTION SETTING, AND BOOSTING THE POWER OF YOUR SPELLS.

AMETHYST: THIS GORGEOUS PURPLE STONE IS ALL ABOUT INTUITION AND PROTECTION. AMETHYST HELPS TO CALM THE MIND, MAKING IT GREAT FOR MEDITATION, DREAM WORK, AND KEEPING THOSE PESKY NEGATIVE ENERGIES AT BAY. IT'S LIKE A CHILL PILL AND A PROTECTIVE SHIELD, ALL IN ONE!

ROSE QUARTZ: THE "STONE OF LOVE," ROSE QUARTZ IS ESSENTIAL FOR SELF-LOVE, HEALING, AND ATTRACTING POSITIVE RELATIONSHIPS. IT'S A GENTLE, NURTURING CRYSTAL THAT OPENS THE HEART CHAKRA, LIKE A WARM HUG FOR YOUR SOUL.

BLACK TOURMALINE: IF YOU'RE LOOKING FOR PROTECTION, THIS IS THE CRYSTAL TO HAVE. BLACK TOURMALINE CREATES AN ENERGETIC SHIELD AROUND YOU, REPELLING NEGATIVE ENERGY AND KEEPING YOU GROUNDED. IT'S LIKE HAVING YOUR OWN PERSONAL BODYGUARD, ALWAYS THERE TO WATCH YOUR BACK.

CITRINE: KNOWN FOR ITS SUNNY, VIBRANT ENERGY, CITRINE IS THE CRYSTAL OF ABUNDANCE AND MANIFESTATION. IT HELPS ATTRACT SUCCESS AND PROSPERITY, MAKING IT A FAVORITE FOR WITCHES FOCUSED ON MANIFESTING THEIR DREAMS. IT'S LIKE A LITTLE LUCKY CHARM THAT REMINDS YOU THAT ANYTHING IS POSSIBLE.

Expanding Your Collection: Let Your Intuition Guide You

As you grow in your practice, you'll naturally want to expand your crystal collection. But don't feel rushed—building a crystal toolkit is a personal and gradual journey. It's like collecting your favorite band's albums—you start with the classics and then slowly add to your collection as you discover new favorites. You can start by adding crystals that call to you or that align with specific intentions or rituals. Crystals like Labradorite (for magic and intuition), Carnelian (for confidence and creativity), or Selenite (for cleansing and peace) are excellent choices as you develop your craft. When you feel a particular crystal calling your name in a shop, trust your intuition—that's often a sign that the crystal has something special to offer you.

Crystal Storage: Show Off Your Sparkly Treasures!

Once you start collecting crystals, you'll want to think about how to store and display them. There's no "right" way, so let your creativity flow! Some witches like to store their crystals in wooden boxes or velvet pouches to keep them safe and protected. Others love to display them on altars, shelves, or even small glass dishes to create a magical atmosphere in their room. You might even set up a crystal grid on your windowsill where the sunlight or moonlight can charge your stones. The key is to keep them in a space where you can easily access and connect with their energy. It's like creating a mini crystal sanctuary!

Using Crystals in Rituals: Power Up Your Magic!

Crystals aren't just for collecting—they're tools that you can use to enhance your rituals and spells. It's like adding special effects to your magical movie! One of the simplest ways to incorporate crystals into your magic is to place them on your altar or hold them in your hand while performing a spell. For example, if you're doing a love spell, place Rose Quartz on your altar to amplify the loving energy. Or if you're performing a protection ritual, hold Black Tourmaline in your hand to shield yourself from negativity.

You can also use crystals to create elixirs—infusions of water charged with the energy of the crystal. It's like making a magical potion! To make a crystal elixir, start by placing a clean crystal in a glass of purified water (make sure the crystal is water-safe—some stones, like Selenite, dissolve in water). Leave the glass in sunlight or moonlight for a few hours to charge the water with the crystal's energy. You can then drink the elixir (if the crystal is safe for consumption) or use it to anoint yourself, your magical tools, or your space. Always research your crystals to ensure they're non-toxic before making an elixir!

Crystals also work beautifully with other magical tools like candles, herbs, and incense. It's like creating a symphony of magical energies! For example, you can place a crystal near a burning candle to amplify the candle's intention. If you're working with herbs, consider pairing crystals with similar properties—for instance, pairing Amethyst with lavender for calming energy or Citrine with basil for abundance and success. The more you experiment, the more you'll discover how these energies blend together to create even more powerful magic.

Customizing Your Toolkit: Make it Uniquely Yours

As your practice grows, you'll find that your connection to certain crystals deepens. This is your personal magic evolving, and your crystal toolkit should reflect that. Selecting crystals that resonate with your unique journey is an important part of customizing your toolkit. It's like creating a playlist of your favorite songs—it's all about what speaks to *you*.

For example, if you feel drawn to the moon's energy, you might want to include Moonstone or Labradorite in your collection. If personal healing is your focus, Rose Quartz and Amazonite might become your go-to stones. You don't have to follow anyone else's path—create rituals that feel right for you. For example, if you enjoy journaling, you can hold a crystal while you write, letting its energy guide your thoughts. Or if you're into dream work, you might place Amethyst or Selenite under your pillow to enhance your dreams. The beauty of witchcraft is that it's a deeply personal practice, and your crystal toolkit is a reflection of your unique energy and goals.

Crystals can also be used for special occasions and life transitions. If you're celebrating a birthday or a new beginning, consider using Citrine or Sunstone to welcome fresh energy and joy. During times of stress or transition, grounding stones like Smoky Quartz or Hematite can offer support. By incorporating crystals into significant moments in your life, you create a powerful connection between your personal milestones and your magical practice.

Unlocking Your Crystal Potential

Becoming a Crystal Whisperer!

S o, you've built your crystal toolkit, you're learning the ropes of witchcraft, and you're starting to feel that magical connection with your crystals. Now, it's time to take things to the next level and unlock the full potential of your sparkly allies! Working with crystals is more than just collecting pretty stones – it's about deepening your connection to their energies, expanding your knowledge, and trusting yourself to use them in magical and meaningful ways. In this chapter, we'll explore how to grow your crystal practice, trust your intuition, and embrace crystals as lifelong companions on your witchcraft journey.

Expanding Your Crystal Knowledge: Become a Crystal Nerd!

One of the coolest things about crystals is that there's *always* more to learn. Even if you've mastered the basics, there's a whole world of crystal knowledge out there waiting for you to explore. It's like discovering a hidden treasure trove of secrets and superpowers!

A great way to deepen your understanding of crystals is by diving into books and resources that offer expert guidance. Some fantastic reads to get you started include *The Crystal Bible* by Judy Hall, which is like the ultimate crystal encyclopedia, and *Crystals for Healing* by Karen Frazier, which focuses on how crystals can help you feel your best.

But books are just the beginning! In today's world, you can also connect with crystal enthusiasts and witches online. It's like having a global coven at your fingertips! Platforms like Instagram, TikTok, and Reddit are full of crystal lovers who post about their favorite stones, crystal grids, and rituals. Don't be shy—join the conversation! You'll find that sharing your journey with others helps you grow faster and adds even more magic to your crystal practice. It's like having a group chat with your magical besties.

As you explore deeper into the world of crystals, you might feel drawn to try new and rare crystals. Maybe you've already worked with classics like Amethyst and Rose Quartz, but what about crystals like Moldavite, which is known for its powerful transformative energy, or Shungite, a rare stone said to help shield against electromagnetic radiation? Trying out new crystals can open you up to different energies and expand your abilities as a witch. It's like adding new skills to your magical repertoire! When experimenting with new crystals, always take it slow—allow yourself time to connect with the crystal and feel how its energy interacts with your own. It's like getting to know a new friend.

Trusting Your Intuition: Your Inner Compass

If there's one thing that will take your crystal practice to the next level, it's learning to trust your intuition. When you work with crystals, it's not just about memorizing facts—it's about feeling the energy, tuning in to what the crystal is telling you, and trusting that inner voice that guides your magical practice. Developing confidence in your crystal work can take time, but the more you trust yourself, the stronger your magic becomes. It's like flexing your intuition muscle!

One of the best ways to trust your intuition is to start by simply *listening* to your crystals. Crystals have a way of "speaking" to us, not in words, but in energy, feelings, and impressions. For example, when you hold a crystal in your hand, close your eyes and ask it what it wants to help you with. You might feel a warm sensation, a tingle, or even an emotional shift. These subtle signs are your crystal communicating with you. Practice this regularly, and you'll start to notice how different crystals give you different feelings or messages. It's like learning a new language, but instead of words, it's all about vibes.

Another way to strengthen your intuition is by incorporating crystals into your daily routine. Building a daily practice around your crystals not only enhances your connection with them but also helps you become more attuned to their energy. You can start with something simple, like choosing a crystal each morning based on how you feel or what energy you want to bring into your day. Carry it with you, meditate with it, or even keep it on your desk as a reminder of your intentions. The more often you work with your crystals, the easier it becomes to trust yourself when you're using them for rituals, spells, or healing.

Crystals as a Lifelong Tool: Your Magical BFFs

Crystals are more than just temporary tools—they're lifelong companions that evolve with you as you grow on your magical journey. One of the most amazing things about crystals is that their energy can shift and change as *you* do. A crystal that you worked with as a beginner might offer you new insights as you advance, or a stone that once felt "meh" might suddenly resonate with you after a big life change. It's like having friends who grow and change with you.

For example, you might have started with Clear Quartz for clarity and focus, but over time, you might discover that it also helps you tap into deeper spiritual practices, like manifestation or astral projection. Your crystals grow with you, supporting you at every stage of your magical and personal development. This is why it's so important to maintain the energy of your crystals over time, like taking care of your besties.

To keep your crystals effective and energized in the long term, regular care is essential. Just like your phone needs a recharge, your crystals need regular cleansing and recharging to stay at their best. Use methods like moonlight charging, smudging with sage, or placing them on a Selenite slab to refresh their energy. Pay attention to how your crystals feel—if they start to feel dull or less vibrant, it might be time for a little extra TLC.

Finally, as you grow in your crystal practice, think about how you can pass on this knowledge and magic to others. Sharing your crystals and experiences can be incredibly rewarding, whether it's through teaching a friend how to use crystals or gifting a loved one a stone that's helped you on your journey. By passing on your knowledge, you're not only helping others unlock their crystal potential, but you're also creating a legacy of magic that lasts beyond you.

Embrace the Magic!

Crystals are magical companions that help us through every stage of life. By expanding your knowledge, trusting your intuition, and taking care of your crystals, you're setting yourself up for a lifelong relationship with these beautiful stones. They'll be with you as you grow, offering guidance, protection, and inspiration. So keep your heart open, your crystals charged, and your magic flowing!

CLOSING REFLECTIONS

Y ou've made it! We've journeyed through the wonders of crystals together, exploring their magical properties, their ability to enhance our emotional and spiritual lives, and how they can help manifest our deepest desires. But the magic doesn't end here. In fact, this is only the beginning. Crystals are lifelong companions, constantly evolving with us as we grow, learn, and change. Now that you've unlocked the power of crystals, the next step is to take this knowledge and make it your own.

TRUST YOUR INTUITION

If there's one thing I hope you take away from this book, it's the importance of trusting your intuition. You are a unique witch with your own magical path, and no two people will ever experience crystals in exactly the same way. The beauty of working with crystals is that they help us tap into our own energy, our own feelings, and our own power. Your intuition will always be your best guide when it comes to selecting, using, and caring for crystals.

Throughout these chapters, you've learned techniques for choosing the right crystal, cleansing and charging it, creating grids, and using crystals for emotional healing, protection, and manifestation. You now have a toolkit of powerful resources at your disposal. But remember, this is your magic. Don't be afraid to experiment. Some of the most incredible discoveries come from trying new things and following your instincts. If a crystal calls to you in a way that isn't covered in this book, go ahead and explore it. Your intuition will lead you to the right practices.

CRYSTALS AS LIFELONG ALLIES

Crystals are not just magical tools—they are lifelong allies. They will be there for you in moments of joy, offering extra sparkle and light to your celebrations. They'll be there when you need support, offering grounding energy to help you through tough times. And they'll be there when you simply need to connect with yourself and reflect. As you grow and change, so will your relationship with crystals. A stone that resonates with you today might take on a new meaning or energy a year from now, and that's the magic of it. Crystals evolve with us, reflecting our own inner transformations.

Remember, you don't need a massive collection to tap into the power of crystals. A small, carefully chosen selection of stones can be just as powerful as an entire shelf full. What matters is the connection you build with them. The more time you spend working with your crystals—whether through meditation, manifestation, or simply carrying them with you—the deeper that bond will become.

SHARING THE MAGIC

One of the most rewarding parts of working with crystals is sharing their magic with others. You might find yourself gifting a friend a Rose Quartz for self-love, creating a crystal grid for a family member in need of protection, or teaching a sibling how to cleanse and charge their first stone. Crystals have a way of bringing people together, and sharing what you've learned is a beautiful way to spread the magic.

If you ever feel stuck or like your crystal journey is at a standstill, remember that there is always more to learn. The world of crystals is vast and endlessly fascinating. You can dive deeper into their geological origins, study how different cultures have used crystals throughout history, or explore more advanced practices like using crystals in astral travel or dreamwork. There is no limit to how far you can go with your crystal practice.

CRYSTALS AS A REFLECTION OF YOU

Perhaps the most magical thing about crystals is how they reflect what's already within you. Every crystal amplifies something inside you—whether it's your confidence, your intuition, or your compassion. When you work with crystals, you're not simply using an external tool. You're tapping into your own energy, your own power. Crystals are here to remind you that you already have everything you need inside you to create magic in your life. They simply help you see it more clearly.

As you continue your crystal journey, take time to reflect on how far you've come. Think about the first time you held a crystal in your hand and compare it to where you are now. How have you grown? What have you learned about yourself? Crystals are more than just stones—they are mirrors that show us our own growth and potential. The more you work with them, the more you will see your own magic reflected back at you.

YOUR NEXT STEPS

Now that you have a solid foundation in crystal magic, it's time to take that knowledge into the world. Try incorporating crystals into your daily life. Carry one in your pocket or place a few around your home. Use them during meditation, or simply hold one when you need a little extra calm or focus. Remember that crystals are versatile—they can be used in countless ways, and part of the fun is discovering what works best for you.

As you move forward, keep an open mind and a playful spirit. Magic is meant to be joyful, and working with crystals should feel fun and exciting. Don't worry if something doesn't click right away—sometimes the magic unfolds slowly, revealing itself over time. Trust the process, trust your crystals, and most importantly, trust yourself.

You've unlocked the power of crystals, and now the magic is in your hands. Keep exploring, keep experimenting, and keep shining your light. The world is full of magic, and you are a part of it.

About the Author

In *The Little Witch* series, Wilhelmina Woods has crafted a delightful collection of 5 guidebooks designed especially for little witches aged 7 to 11. These compact guides gently lead children on a journey to discover the magic within their hearts. Whether it's learning about Animal Companions, nurturing Magical Plants, or growing Herbs, each book offers something enchanting for every little witch. These guides are a perfect introduction to opening their hearts, to the wonders of the witchy world.

For young Witches aged 12 to 16, Wilhelmina has carefully created another set of 5 guidebooks, tailored to help them on their path of self-discovery. These books are ideal companions as they navigate their teenage years, offering wisdom and guidance on embracing their inner magic.

As they grow older, there are 5 more books designed for Teenage Witches aged 16 to 19, helping them fully embrace their witchiness, find empowerment, and claim their Witch Heart.

And for the adults? Wilhelmina has everything covered. A stepping stone into the true witch heart has been carefully created, inspiring the beginner Witch to become the witch they were always meant to be.

ABOUT WILHELMINA WOODS

Wilhelmina Woods hails from a rich lineage of Witches, Healers, Shamans, and Wise Women on both her mother's and father's sides, with the occasional nun adding a surprising twist to her family tree. Raised in an openly spiritual home alongside her four younger sisters, she was always encouraged to embrace her true self. For Wilhelmina, this meant wholeheartedly embracing her Witch heritage. Her sisters—River, Sage, Raven and Willow—are also authors, each following their own unique path. Wilhelmina, with pride and passion, carries on the family's magical legacy.

www.ingramcontent.com/pod-product-compliance
Lightning Source LLC
Chambersburg PA
CBHW062005040426
42447CB00010B/1926